# Petals of Laughter

# Enid Thwaites

Published by Woodlark Publishing
Copyright © Enid Thwaites 2015
ISBN-13: 978-0-9933491-2-6

## Acknowledgements:

Many thanks to:
Suzan Collins of Get Writing who after attending her workshop inspired me to write this collection of humorous anecdotes which helped me and my daughter through difficult times.

Richard and Gina of the Coconut Loft Art Gallery and Coffee Lounge for their support in providing practical advice on the blurb for my book.

Jill and Philip who found quotes suitable for my book

Cover: Jen Moon

## Dedication:

This book is dedicated
to Alan and Andy without whom this
book would not have been possible. And
to Helen without whom I would not
have written anything.

Alan

Andy

Helen

# Contents page

## Sombreros on Board

We had enjoyed our holiday and had evidence in the form of two beautiful Sombreros which had to be worn on the flight home so the boys sat together.

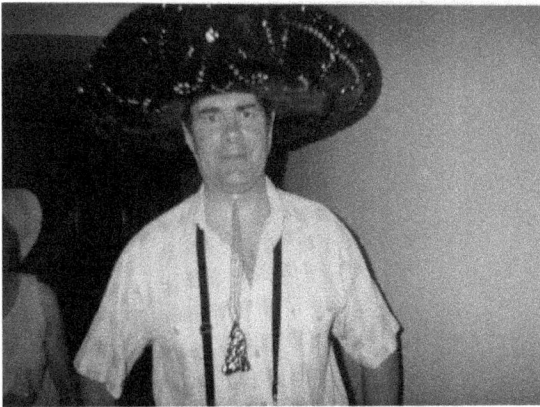

Andy found a Mr Bean film on the in-flight movie and Alan settled in next to him to enjoy the jokes. So did the entire plane! Most people would like to have slept, but this was not possible with the loud laughter issuing from my boys! In the end the whole plane gave up and enjoyed Mr Bean with Andy and Alan.

## Camel Ride at 45°

We went to a Bedouin feast on our honeymoon. We were warned not to imbibe too much food or drink as it was somewhat basic! Mike and Alan ignored the advice and imbibed freely all set before them. Soon they were happily unaware of any problems. Seeing their happy state, they were offered a ride on a camel. As they scrambled aboard the padded saddle slipped precariously to a 45° angle. The Arab increased the speed of the camel thinking the boys would fall off. No, nothing removed them or depressed their mood.

On returning to the hotel Mike's wife and I left our husbands to sleep it off in the flower beds in the foyer.

## Uncle Charlie Rides a Tandem

My uncle Charlie was my Mum's brother and was opposite to her in all ways. Mum was gentle, careful and thought carefully before she acted, he, on the other hand, jumped in with both feet without careful consideration.

Dad was a lorry driver and on one of his journey's saw two young people having a most uncomfortable ride along the A12 on a tandem. He stopped to see if he could help and was amazed to find that Uncle Charlie was one and Auntie Joan was the other.

Auntie Joan was always willing to try any exciting adventure, but was finding this journey difficult to say the least. Auntie Joan is blind and by the time Dad picked them up they had stuffed the tyres with straw having suffered several punctures, and progress was extremely slow and exhausting. I think they were very pleased to have a lift back!

## The Master and the Cakes

The Master suffered from a complaint which required that he consumed sugary foods on a regular basis. Andy noticed two rather delicious iced doughnuts on the desk and enquired if he was going to auction them off at the end of the lesson. The master replied that he was not, but if Andy came and saw him at the end of the lesson he could have one for his cheek provided that he sat in the dining room to eat it. He did!

"God will fill thy mouth with laughing and thy lips with rejoicing."

Job 8 v 20-21

# Cheese and Biscuits

It was a difficult time when my Mum and Dad needed me to care for them and Alan felt lonely when it became necessary, after Dad died, to move in and care completely for Mum. He stayed at home but became more and more stressed with only the cat for company.

He had been particularly upset one evening as we were leaving getting very irate about the situation and hoping to alleviate this I had prepared his usual snack of cheese and biscuits. Suddenly the angry voice stopped and a slightly plaintive tone followed us out of the door 'And now the cats got the cheese and biscuits.' Poor Alan it really had not been his day.

15

# Sailor Suit

My Dad was Welsh. Brought up in the Rhonda Valley his playground often included a coal tip or two.

A maiden Aunt was coming to tea and so Dad and his brothers and sister had been scrubbed up ready to meet her. They duly appeared to be kissed and given their presents. Dad's was a white sailor suit, which he duly put on and was admired in. As the afternoon progressed the adults wanted to talk so the children were ushered out to play. Dad found his friends and off they went. He was wearing his sailor suit when he left the house to play with his friends. Needless to say the suit did not stay its proper shade and neither did Dad. On returning home at the due time Dad knocked politely on the door, but when the maiden aunt opened it she exclaimed, 'Whose this – I don't know you, go away you dirty little boy.' 'But I'm George – look I'm wearing your present.' She took some convincing but eventually let him in.

# Grandad and the Door Creaked Open

As a young man my father got very interested in horror movies and stories. He was the kindest and gentlest man you could ever meet but I think that young men enjoy the shuddering nature of most of them. One evening he was sitting alone at home in Wales and the radio was on 'The Monkey's Paw.' In through the creaking door came … THE CAT.

# Uncle Charlie's Tyre

When Uncle Charlie was young he must have been as quick to wear out his shoes as Andy was. His Mum began to despair at finding anything that would prolong the life of his shoes. She was a widow by this time and money was not available for renewal or even repair, when suddenly she had a good idea. Charlie had brought home yet another tyre to take out and race with his mates – that might work. She brought it in and found the sharpest knife to cut out new soles and heels for Charlie's boots. By the time he needed to wear them in the morning they were strong enough to with stand the hardest wear and Charlie rather liked his new boots until the weekend when he went to look for his tyre, and found it in a rather depleted state.

'What have you done mum, that was my best tyre!'

'Well now it's on your best shoes, sorry old chap.'

## Bullying and Doctor

Andy's GP was a father of two sons himself and so was understanding of the difficulties of boys at school. Andy had suffered quite a few kicks and punches, with quite painful bruising. I was determined to ask the Doctor about these when I took Andy to have his bruised black thumbnail removed.

My memory was not good even then and I forgot to check about the bruising which was in an uncomfortable place.

'Good job you forgot mum he might have cut that off!'

When later Grandad had to go for his M.O.T. he challenged the doctor.

'What's this about you upsetting and frightening my grandson?'

'Oh no I didn't mean to do that. What was wrong?'

Grandad explained the dilemma and he did not think that the doctor would ever stop laughing.

## Mr and Mrs

Alan and I went to a social evening with Waveney Light Opera Group (W.L.O.G ) a few months after our wedding and the organiser suggested that we play the new T.V. game of Mr & Mrs devised to find out just what you don't know.

When asked the colour of my eyes he insisted they were blue. I'm afraid they are brown.

## The Incredible Hulk

When Andy was five it was a very hot summer and a friend and neighbour called on me to invite me into her beautiful garden for tea with some of the neighbours. Unfortunately I was unable to relax in the summer July sunshine on this particular occasion as I had to ice the Incredible Hulk – a birthday cake for Andy complete with green body, black shorts and a pink shirt!

## A Tank to the Toy Service

Andy's favourite toy was a tank – plastic and well used. We used to give other needy children presents at Christmas and were asked to bring just one favourite from each child. Once again all of London Road was roused by my son this time trundling a tank to and this time into church right to the front to present it to the minister who was duly surprised and deafened.

## Sitting in the Doorway

After his accident, in which he sustained a severe brain injury, Andy was supposed not to be capable of formal thought but one day, I needed to go to the toilet and moved to go.

Andy positioned his chair in the door way and turned on the tap roaring with laughter – how's that for formal thought.

## Chocolate Biscuit

Helen and Andy developed early on a liking for chocolate biscuits. Helen had a sensible method of eating it – putting her thumb only on the chocolate side.

When the biscuit was finished she just licked her thumb, no mess no worry.

Andy, on the other hand, used various holds which distributed the chocolate into his hair, ears, nose, over knees, and over the box I sat him in.

How to decorate the immediate area and self with a one sided chocolate biscuit – he was the expert.

## Billy the Stink

Billy was one of our first baby ferrets. From the beginning he was intent on following his own individual way. He loved his food just like Andy and was not happy being locked in his hutch.

Before his eyes opened he was falling down the ladder from the nest where he was born.

Andy would allow him to play in the garden but he was more interested in coming into the house which did not seem too bad until someone stood on his tail and suddenly the room was filled with the worst smell you could imagine.

A skunk would have difficulties reaching that long lasting stink, three days it took to subside.

Needless to say Billy was not a welcome visitor after that.

## The Pink Cello

It was in a production of Orpheus in the Underworld with the Waveney Light Opera Group. Alan was one of the naughty school children, who had to play instruments. His instrument was large and very pink. A cello which had no strings but this was certainly an advantage for the audience.

Alan's musical knowledge was limited to head chorister in church, no instrumental skill – but pink that was insult to injury – he hated pink!

## The Three Hour Costume

Helen had become a regular participant in local craft fairs. One of her favourites was one held at Raveningham (a village near Beccles in Suffolk) each year.

She had been quite busy and had completely forgotten that the stall holders had decided to dress up in costume for a country fair, in period costume. Remembering this later on the Friday evening there was no chance to hire or buy a costume.

Panic not. I can do this! Pink material was found which was just big enough to work. A paper pattern cut, the material soon followed.

Stitching began, no time to tack. Hem finished in record time. Praise be it fitted!

Off she went in the morning wearing her homespun dress.

When she came home she had won first prize for her fancy dress. I felt quite pleased - so did she.

## Billy and the Malteser

We were on the way to the church bazaar. This was an event which brought all the family together. Andy was quite keen to come because he could buy Granddad's pickled onions and I might forget.

Andy had Billy (the ferret) on his harness, and, for once, Billy was enjoying the walk in spite of the noisy traffic. In the gutter Billy made a discovery, a malteser, which he impaled on his tooth. Not the usual food for a ferret. Andy retrieved it after a short struggle. At which point Billy refused to walk another inch, neither did he want anything to do with Andy for the rest of the day.

Helen carried Billy the rest of the way and subsequently at the bazaar, where his mood improved with lots of fuss and admiration from many elderly ladies whose brothers had kept ferrets in their youth. One person, however, did not want to meet Billy, the minister kept a respectful distance, not quite trusting his happy nature. But Billy never bit any one; he looked on himself as an entertaining member of the family.

# Frogs

Andy had asked some of his friends to his birthday party when he was six. This was the last one in our house as they preferred a bigger area to let off steam.

They all went into the garden to do a treasure hunt which soon turned into a frog hunt as the neighbour had a pond from which the froglets would gravitate to our more Wildlife setting.

When the boys had scrubbed up they sat down and had soon consumed all but the cake which had place of honour on the table. Of course it did – it was a football. I took the large knife in my hand and said,

'I shall have to be careful how I cut this.'

'Oh please don't hurt the little frogs.' said a very worried little boy.

'No, look, there is something else inside.'

In fact there was a small plastic football for each of the boys' presents.

I'd had to remove the centre of the cake as it had been a little undercooked in the middle.

## The Dietary Habits of Youth

Food was always popular with Andy. One afternoon when meeting big sister Helen from school Andy was found to have consumed a whole punnet of raspberries and half a punnet of strawberries, plus three whole pickled onions when he reached Grandad's house – I didn't blame him they were good! However, not wise on top of all that fruit, His tummy never suffered any upset – miraculously.

## Determination Pre Birth

Andy the determined young man was ever this – from his very conception he was conceived whilst precautions were taken.

"He was born with a gift of laughter."
Rafael Sabatini 1875-1950

## Happy Christening Day

At the christening, Andy laughed and enjoyed even the loudest hymn. No tears for him on his christening.

## Happy Clamour

Olly was a plastic ride on toy which Andy found an asset in his journey time, and great fun to make a really loud crunching noise in transit – bad enough to waken the heaviest sleeper, as Andy passed the houses on his way to church on a Sunday morning.

## Follow that Sound

Andy was a lively child, never wanting the pram to stop, and when he had started to move himself about he never wanted to go back into it.

He developed a deceptive jog trot that moved him to destinations quicker than seemed possible.

On a visit to Norwich Castle he was retrieved numerous times by the security guard having set every animal sound recording going continuously.

# Golden Wedding When Charlotte Died

A sad ending necessitated Helen's tears and Andy laughing and chanting, 'Charlotte died. Charlotte died,' all on the way to the restaurant. And by the way, he was not pristine when we got there but Helen certainly cheered me up! She was immaculate but all Andy was interested in was the food.

# Our Best Man Unmarried Me after My Wedding

I had re-joined my singing group and was given the part of Casilda in The Gondoliers. Graham Smith had the programme printed and lo and behold I was Enid Westwood again, five months after I became Mrs Thwaites with him as our best man.

## Andy Makes a Bed for Matthew

Andy always made room for his friends at home. When he was first at school, a friend asked if I would look after her little boy while she returned to work. This was discussed in the family and seemed like a good idea. After a few days Andy wanted Matthew to stay the night.

'But Andy there is just not enough room.'

Upstairs he went and I could hear ominous sounds of removal and rearrangement. As soon as I could I went upstairs to see what arrangements had been made.

'But where will he sleep, Andrew?' and then I saw a tell-tale pillow protruding over the top of the wardrobe.

'How is he going to get up and down and, more importantly not fall off?'

Needless to say he did not stay overnight.

Sometime later on a family holiday Andy chose the top bunk in the caravan. It was not many minutes before he fell out – in fact it happened seventeen times before he could be persuaded that the bottom bunk was a safer idea for him Helen, bless her, never fell out!

# Birthday Embarrassment in EDP*

It was Andy's birthday – he had been out with his friends and they came back with him to help him demolish his birthday cake.

Very quiet, concentrating on eating, Alan did not realise they were there and appeared stark naked to show me something he had found in the EDP. Realising his mistake he backed out behind the EDP and fled upstairs again.

Quietly Andy's friend said, 'Local councillor exposed in the EDP!'

I'm afraid we laughed.

*Eastern Daily Press newspaper

## Christmas

Christmas was always especially exciting for Andy. For many years he found sleep almost impossible on Christmas Eve.

'Has he been yet?' was the phrase that continued on into the very latest of nights to early morning.

'No and he won't come until you go to sleep.'

'I'm asleep mum, I'm asleep!'

'No you're not or you would not be talking to me.'

Eventually the calling out would abate and I would have a few minutes in which to put the pillow cases into his room before he was awake again.

'Mum! He's been!'

'Yes you can open just one.' Of course my request fell on deaf ears and sometime later I found his presents surrounded by many torn paper wrappings still attached to their tags, parted, irreparably from its present which had been given. How would we manage 'Thank you' letters?

Andy was happy having opened them all well before dawn!

## Yeoman of the Guard

Alan, Helen and I were asked to take part in a production of the above in Norwich. Not wishing to leave Andrew out we included him as the headsman.

'Alright,' he said, 'as long as nobody knows who I am.'

It evidently was not a cool thing to be associated with. He quite liked the costume, black with its cover all mask.

Unfortunately the programme organiser did not know the rule and Andy was named as the headsman, he only forgave us grudgingly when the other young girls vied with each other for his attention during the production 'Where's Charlotte?' 'I think she is round the other side.' 'She's with Andrew!' and the second Charlotte sped to the other side.

Later on Andy told me that he had had enough of girlfriends – he preferred a harem.

"Then our mouth filled with laughter
and our tongue with singing."
Psalms 126 v 2

## A Little Girl's Favourite Song

On a bus journey to Great Yarmouth with Andy and Helen a little girl was sitting on the seat just in front of us with her mother. She had seen the view out of the window and had decided to practice her musical skills. Unfortunately the only song she knew did not bear repeating, 'These boots are made for walking and that's just what they'll do, one of these days these boots are going to all walk

All

Over

You!

The slide in the tune was emphasised. Andy believed in encouraging little children so he clapped at the end. Once again we were treated to what was nearly the right tune and the slide at the end got steeper and again, and again, and again even the applause had long stopped.

The little girl's mum was so embarrassed but I'm afraid the serenade was carried on till the end of the journey.

I think it may have continued but we took a different route!

## Permission to Shock You Mum

Andy was the only one in my family blessed with curly hair. It grew into flowing locks which many admired.

One day, quite out of the blue a strange young man appeared on the doorstep with what was called a No 2 haircut.

Criminal from prison was the title I would have given it but gone were the flowing locks for good.

## Let Down by a Handle

It was a beautiful day for a lovely wedding and Dad wanted to stand tall for the grandson he had brought up as his own.

It was an R.A.F wedding and military precision was the order of the day.

On the steps of the church in the centre of London Dad stood with the rest. No stick to support him but hidden behind the mighty pillar which supported the building the handle protruding, as if to remind us we all need support.

## On The Bus to Woburn

We were on the way to Bryan's wedding at Woburn Abbey.

A beautiful journey prompted by Andy seeking his gun to take aim at the venison in the park. Yes, Andy's humour was present in all circumstances.

He was so happy that day, his food was perfectly presented in a meal which was exactly the same as ours only creamed to a consistency perfect for him to eat and enjoy.

That evening he danced the night away on legs so crippled! What a joy for him.

## Sandwiches

I had to be in hospital for a few days for a minor opp. Alan did try to take care of the children's needs but found lunch sandwiches beyond his capabilities.

On their arrival at my parent's home before going off to school Mum checked the contents of their lunch boxes and immediately sent Dad over to the shops to buy some bread.

'Those poor little things can't eat these!'

The bread slices being so uneven that the contents were deposited around the box. Not his finest effort. But as Dad said, 'The Boy Tried'.

"He that sitteth in the Heavens shall laugh."
Psalm 2 v 4

## Ghosts and Electricity

Andy had brought his friends back to Mum's house. The room had been cleared as mum had died and the house was for sale.

The group said how lovely it was to have a space where they could sit, relax and chat. A new carpet was all there was to sit on – but, leaning on the walls they were fine.

Andy liked to spook people with ghost stories and was holding court when Helen gently pressed the light switch behind her head – the light dimmed and went out and something like real fear crept into the room. Not for long – Helen admitted her prank and switched the light back on. Fortunately everyone laughed.

## How the Mighty Have Fallen

Nineteen churches we visited that day. I had been laughed at frequently because of a squeak that had got louder the further I went on my tricycle.

The weather was perfect and I was enjoying the view; when glancing up at the road ahead, I realise that Helen has disappeared.

'Helen' I call and a plaintive voice replies, 'I'm here'. Still she is invisible and then I can see her desperately trying to climb out of a deep ditch at the side of the road ahead. As I helped her up and rescued her bike – we laughed together at our eventful ride.

## Andy and Alan Upstage Roy Waller Local Radio Presenter

It was carnival time again and as usual Alan was participating as well as organising. It was a fancy dress competition with Roy Waller a local radio presenter 'in charge'.

Roy always seemed to win the day in any on stage interview/conversation, but not this one!

Alan and Andy went on stage as Del Boy and Rodney from Fools and Horses. Yes out of his pocket Del (Alan) took a flimsy pair of Helen's panties pink and black, 'Give these to Delories with my compliments' said Alan – for once Roy could think of nothing to say!

An extraordinary thing for him.

## Rose and Cake to Prince Edward

It was an exciting time, Prince Edward came to Beccles and it was Andy's birthday.

'I'll give him some of my cake,' ever the generous soul. Andy stood full of expectancy as the car came slowly towards us.

The photographer was someone I was at school with – seeing Helen with a beautiful red rose and Andy with a carefully covered piece of birthday cake, ushered them forward and took a lovely picture of the presentation which figured in the press next day.

"God made me laugh, so that all who
hear will laugh with me."
Gen 21 v 6

## Billy Connelly Impersonations

Andy's favourite comedian was Billy Connelly, He had the same sense of humour and Andy got really good at mimicking his Scottish accent and his jokes. In fact I could better understand his version than that of his hero.

Helen's friend liked Andy's imitations and said that when he recovered sufficiently to repeat them she would come and visit him. Unfortunately he never could, but many things he did manage.

## Bite Detector on Bike Wheel

Andy would escape to fish if he could and this one evening he was fishing in a very dark area with no street lights.

Having just left the bright lights of town, our eyes were not accustomed to the semi darkness.

We called out to Andy as a cycle approached with only the tiniest flashing light on the front wheel.

No one answered our call but the black bike approached through the semi darkness.

When the bike was almost on us a voice boomed 'Boo!' It was Andy but he certainly had us worried.

## Dayglow Orange

It was that time again when the Opera Group publicity took priority. Alan was expecting a call from the Printers about the posters and flyers and so everyone had to cut their telephone calls short, very short.

At last the call came through and suddenly Alan developed an emphasised plum in his mouth!

Andy thought this very funny.

'Why did you put on such a posh voice Dad?' he asked.

'It's my business voice.'

'I didn't know you had one – dayglow orange – Dad honestly!' Andy replied.

Andy collapsed in fits of laughter at his 'posh dayglow orange Dad!'

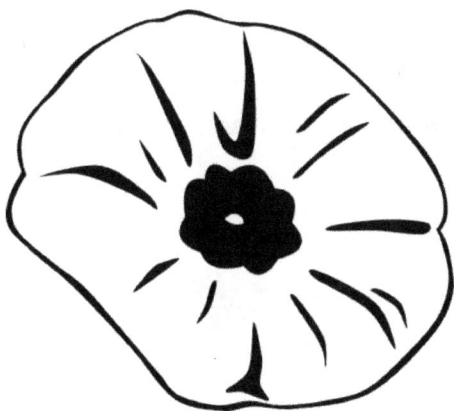

## Drunken Interview with a Coat

Alan treated us to an amusing one way conversation with a coat. He returned from yet another Rugby Club celebration – ignored us and was really very polite to Andy's yellow puffa jacket hanging in the doorway to air.

'Hello yellow coat.'

'Yes it is a wonderful evening.'

# Hiccups in Church

Andy was not keen on the quiet attitude which was required for church services. I had to 'Shh' him many times but this was the one time he could blame me for having extremely loud hiccups in church!

After his accident Treetops brought him home on many visits - several of which were for the Christmas Tree festival in the church he had grown up in.

Several of the other people from Treetops came too and we always had a very special day.

On this occasion Treetops had come to the Friday evening switch-on which was always very crowded. Needless to say Andy thoroughly enjoyed the busy atmosphere and seeing many people he knew and had not seen for several years.

We watched the switch-on in town and found the doughnut stall on our way to church. The doughnuts were hot, but that added to their taste. Andy consumed three in quick succession and heat combined to give Andy the most resounding attack of hiccups just as we entered the church.

He looked at me and laughed – of course that did not help!

We progressed slowly round the church accompanied by hiccups – for which I could only blame myself. I bought the doughnuts for him!

## Corner of Sheet

It was a hot summer day when we arrived at the rehab centre in Norwich. Andy had always been warm, even in winter. When we went into reception we were met by a somewhat embarrassed nurse.

'Oh hello, I'm so glad you have come, we have lots of visitors today and Andy just won't cover up.'

We went to his room and there he lay as naked as the day he was born. We closed his door and told him the problem of visitors.

'Please cover up even if it's only a sheet. And if you keep still you won't get so hot.'

He nodded and motioned to me to open the door. I did so and when I turned back I could see what had made Helen laugh. Andy had clutched the tiniest corner of his sheet and was

holding it coyly covering the very barest
essentials!

## Buttermere Walk Divided

It's a long way round the mere and Helen felt the need to keep an eye on both her aging parents.

We set off with great enthusiasm but, as usual, Alan began to pull away, he always enjoyed being in front. Unfortunately, as he sped up, I ran out of steam and slowed. At last Helen decided to keep encouraging me in the hope we would eventually catch up with Alan.

We returned to the car park to find Alan conspicuous by his absence. Panic set in as we spoke to the lady in charge of the car park. No, she had not seen Alan but not to worry too much as there were many walkers all the way around. Her confidence in his safety cheered us a little.

We searched all areas we could think of and returned to the car park to find him finishing *his* ice-cream. We had been too concerned to buy ours! Needless to say – we insisted on finishing ours before we moved on!

## Paper Palm Trees

The only times I saw Alan the worse for drink was associated with the wonderful Rugby Club. Even when he retired from the game itself – he still enjoyed any celebration they had.

An elderly neighbour called one day to ask why we had paper palm trees growing in our garden.

Without looking I knew they were remnants of a New Year's Party at the Rugby Club.

## Where Did You Shove It? Award

We had a Straw Race in Beccles which consisted of following a certain route through the town, transporting on bicycle, wheelbarrows or on your back, a straw bale.

The person who did it the fastest and the one who lost least won prizes, but Alan and his buddy – both councillors – won a special 'Where did you shove it?' certificate – they had very little left!

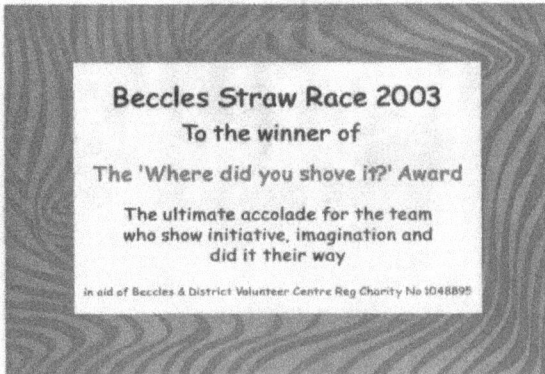

Beccles Straw Race 2003
To the winner of
The 'Where did you shove it?' Award

The ultimate accolade for the team
who show initiative, imagination and
did it their way

in aid of Beccles & District Volunteer Centre Reg Charity No 1048895

## Maurice Danceurse

Alan always enjoyed carnival particularly one year when the twinning committee put in a group of Morris Dancers. The costumes were fairly correct but unfortunately the dancing was not. None of the group really knew what they had to do.

The lady trying to teach them was not given much of a chance. She won one battle however.

'We want sticks'

'No, hankies and bells only, they will do less damage.' she replied.

They danced round the whole Carnival route and at the end, were asked to do it again at another carnival – there is no accounting for taste.

# Dad Lost Them in the Pool

On our family holiday to Bulgaria, Alan was keen to show us his prowess in the pool. Choosing a day when most people had gone out he donned a very skimpy pair of swimming trunks, and plunged into the pool. He did several lengths in his usual enthusiastic manner.

Suddenly the enthusiasm left him and anxious diving ensued.

At last he stood up minus his trunks in fact waving them in the air; fortunately there was nobody else to see him but us.

## We'd Better Go and Make the Bed Dear

Alan's parents had been away in Belgium with friends, and so he had been eating meals with my Mum and Dad and me. Only going home to sleep- that way he did not mess up the kitchen!

We were spending most of our spare time at 'The King's Head' in Beccles along with most of the Waveney Light Opera Group. It was the evening before his parents return and Alan suddenly stood up and announced to the whole company, 'Well I suppose we had better go and make the bed!'

When the laughter had subsided I had to explain that I was going to help make Alan's bed which he had not made for a week in order that he would not upset his mother first day back.

## Helen's Letter

It was Helen's birthday and a very special one because Princess Diana, her favourite Royal, was having a baby and when the baby boy was born Helen was quite disappointed.

'I'll have to write and say how sorry I am that it is a boy!'

'I think that the Princess will be pleased that it is a boy. He will be King one day.'

'No, I'm sure she wanted a girl – a boy is such a nuisance.'

This I think was a consequence of having a younger brother!

The reply which Helen received from the Lady in Waiting confirmed the idea that a boy was most welcome, but she did thank Helen for her kind considerations.

# The Sunday School Class

(A reflective monologue written by my daughter, Helen Thwaites)

As children my brother and I were brought up in a Christian family and attended church and Sunday school regularly. Our mum was one of the teachers and taught the primary class. My brother was frequently bribed to behave himself with sweets, an ice cream, a toy car or some other treat from the corner shop on our way home, and providing he was kept occupied this was largely successful.

This story takes place just after my brother had started nursery in the early 1980's, and through his peers, he had just discovered cap guns. This discovery didn't exactly thrill mum but she decided she would rather know what he was playing with so that she could teach him right from wrong, and hopefully lead him in a better direction.

This particular Sunday morning we had left the main service after the second hymn as we always did, and split into our classes according to our ages. At six years old I was still in the primary class, but thought of myself as `one of the big girls'. My brother who at only just four was, to my mind still `a little boy'. There were seventeen of us in this class and mum was our teacher. I think she found it hard to teach sometimes because the need to be `teacher' for the whole class was made more difficult by having her own children there. I think that this was because her instinct as a mother conflicted with that of a teacher, and she was always trying not to treat us any differently from the other children.

Mum told us all to sit on the floor so that nobody fought over the one red chair that was in the `rainbow room'. She began to tell us a story about how Jesus fed lots of people with very little food. The floor was hard, and our tummies were rumbling because it was nearly lunchtime, so when mum told us how hungry and thirsty the people felt it wasn't hard for us to imagine. ``There were no shops to buy any food and Jesus' friends didn't know how they were going to feed anyone". We were used to this because the majority of shops in Beccles didn't open on Sundays so we couldn't go shopping for food either. ``After a while one of these friends, who was called Andrew, found a little boy who had five loaves and two fish, so what do you think Jesus did?"

With the question asked, my brother could contain himself no longer and, leaping up from the floor, shouted ``Shot him and had the loaves and fishes". Mum sat at the front, went red with embarrassment and gently disciplined her son (also called Andrew) saying ``No that's not how Jesus chose to react" but this was drowned out by the cheers of the other little boys. Trying hard to stay in control of her class mum went on to explain why that was not the case and that Jesus actually shared the food among the people and all had been well fed. ``When the people had finished eating, Jesus' friends tidied up. They collected twelve baskets of leftovers, which amazed everyone." My brother felt that this was a very unsatisfactory outcome, and that his idea was better.

I am glad to say that the story doesn't end there, and that the moral of the story had a long-term effect on my brother as he got older.

As a teenager Andrew became a very keen fisherman, and spent much of his time enjoying this activity. On one of these fishing trips he was thrilled because he caught an 18lb pike, which was his biggest fish ever. With great pride he brought the huge fish home and, holding it up for us to see said, ``it would only take two of these to feed the five thousand wouldn't it mum?" Immediately mum started to laugh and knew that her son had got the right message all those years ago.

Andrew also found an outlet for his endless energy through making bread, and for three years running provided all the bread for the harvest supper. So, looking back I can see that my brother didn't just understand the moral of the story, he lived that moral out in his life and through his enjoyment really did `feed the five thousand'.

## Fire from Heaven –
### Celebration of nine hundred years of Norwich Cathedral

1996 – This was the last big production in which we took part. Alan played multiple roles, while Helen and I were with the death cart for the black death scene. David Lambert did offer to write a part for Andy and his ferret but I think Andy was quite relieved when he didn't!

Our arrival at the theatre to audition for this Celebration was quite amusing. Having arrived at the Theatre Royal we were uncertain of where we should go. We walked to the right side of the theatre and saw a skip. In the skip was a rather dishevelled young man who seemed to be the only person about at that moment. He was busily sorting through the contents of the skip. My husband was unwilling to approach him, but I, being unwilling to turn round and drive home without finding the studio, took my courage in both hands and asked the question.

'Excuse me, could you tell me where the studio is?'

'I'll do better than that, I'll take you myself!'

On arrival at the studio the young man introduced himself as David Lambert, director of the show! This unassuming young man had not only a wonderful sense of humour but a super talent for bringing the cast together and making every rehearsal something to look forward to – great fun!

# Skirt at Mayor Making

My accident happened in 1996 when Alan was deputy Mayor. Unforgettable was the ceremony of mayor making which will live long in my embarrassed memory. Early May and smart clothes were needed. Mother-in-law had kindly made me a long black wrap around skirt which covered all deficiencies. Realising my difficulties of mobility she had fixed it with the then new Velcro. It was not long before I realised the error of depending on this new fitting.

We had all assembled in the beautiful Town Hall of Beccles. Originally built to house only the meetings of the town council, seats have been added around the outside wall. Seats like the theatre ones which spring back against the wall. Fine if you are agile and able to adjust your clothing easily.

The Ceremony began and as Mayoress I had to be presented with a bouquet. Everything went well until I had to stand quickly to receive said beautiful bouquet. I clutched it to my waist as I felt the skirt go loose. The Sergeant-at-Mace advanced to take my bouquet from me and the photographer followed him. 'No thanks' I muttered to The Sergeant-at-Mace. He did not realise how essential was my burden to my dignity.

We found a safety pin as soon as I reached the safety of the Mayor's Chamber. Phew, what a relief – it never actually fell off.

# Mandy Rice – Davies Look Alike

When I was in the sixth form at school, I attended a Discussion Course at Belstead House. In the press the Profumo Scandal was in full flow. I had always wanted to be a blonde and Mandy – Rice Davies was certainly a blonde bombshell. We were given the task of organising a dramatic presentation of an up to date news story. We had the week to prepare! Donning my navy mackintosh belted in tightly  by a wide gold belt, four inch heels and well back brushed (as near blonde as possible) beehive I marched in and played the part. When we finished the applause was enthusiastic but afterwards the lady in charge whispered in my ear, 'You terrified me dear!'

# The Mikado –
# Parts Taken and Reaction

When I first joined The Waveney Light Opera group the second production in The Public Hall was 'The Mikado'. I had the art of Pitti Sing who was a bit of a minx – fine, I enjoyed being a suitable age in the right part. Several years later 'The Mikado' was chosen again. This time at twenty-three I played Katisha, and thoroughly enjoyed being such a powerful individual.

My makeup frightened my nephew, he ran away saying, 'That's not my Aunty Enid!' And Fred, Audrey's elderly husband exclaimed, 'My word she does well for her age!' Fine up to that point, but some years and two children later I played Katisha in a concert. Yes Helen and Andy were treated to my part on a regular basis, it was not until Andy was actually sitting in the audience and saw and heard the chorus' angry reaction that he burst into tears because 'They are being horrible to my mum!' he cried.

He cheered up the next time I appeared in 'The Mikado'. This time as Yum Yum at the tender age of forty-three.

The only thing that cheered me up was the Doyly Carte version had little maids from school even older.

## Song by Helen, Try Singing against it

Alan found learning new songs quite difficult. To build confidence for performance we would be treated to the same song continuously until he got it right. Helen suddenly developed the need to sing a song of her own it began 'Sing a song of Dereham'. The second, third, fourth and fifth were the same – and the same tune.

We still do not know why she sang her song – but Alan went elsewhere to practice.

# Grandad Removes the School Bell Clapper

My father was not the perfect pupil while at school. I think perhaps many people find that the restrictions of scholastic studies do not sit well with most young boys.

Having a walk over the mountain to school one would think that this exercise would suffice.

When Dad arrived at school one day he noticed a ladder left by the painters up to the bell tower. It was too much temptation and encouraged by other early pupils, George, my dad, climbed up and saw his opportunity to ensure that nobody would be late by the bell that day. Gently removing the clapper from the bell and placing it in the bell tower he descended and left the scene. The painter returned soon after and removed the ladder.

All was well until it was time for the headmaster to ring the bell. Nothing – not a tinkle!

Several people were late that day but the punishment was not too severe as he had not taken the clapper away.

## Andy, Wearing His Dad's Shoes, And A Friend go to an All-night Rave

Andy had promised to be home and, of course he wasn't. How could he stay out and be wearing his Dad's best shoes!

Andy's friend's mum called on us early the following morning, with his sister. She had been searching all night wondering where the boys were. We stood on the front step trying to decide what to do next when round the corner came the boys in the car. Sheepishly they walked inside and we began the interrogation – the car broke down in Oulton Broad and they had pushed it all the way home. No, they had been driving it round the corner! They must think we were born yesterday!

**Dear Reader**
If you have enjoyed reading this book,
then please leave a review on Amazon.
Thank you.

## About The Author

Enid is a former primary school teacher and diagnosed Dyslexic. She only found out the reason for her difficulties with both reading and writing when she tried to help her son and he was similarly diagnosed at the age of eight.

A non-fiction writer, Enid enjoys singing, gardening and painting. Her first book, 'Petals of Laughter', includes a collection of humorous anecdotes which helped her through difficult times.

To contact Enid please email her at woodlark44@gmail.com

www.ingramcontent.com/pod-product-compliance
Lightning Source LLC
Chambersburg PA
CBHW070643030426
42337CB00020B/4144